Is de la Société *(E.)*

Fidji *(A.)*

Taiti *(F.)*

the Seasons OF Trans-FORMATiON ARE UPON US...

micheal teal

when i dare to be POWERFUL, to use my STRENGTH in the service of my VISION, then it becomes LESS AND LESS important whether I am AFRAID.

audre lorde

TRANSFORMATION of any kind always exacts a **holy** tussle. he newborn BUTTERFLY struggles to open ITS WINGS so it can conjure up THE STRENGTH to **FLY.** so, too, with **ARTISTS,** INVENTORS, MYSTICS, and **ENTREPRENEURS.**

tama kieves

IF
YOU have yet
to be called
an incorrigible,
DEFIANT
woman,
DONT
WORRY,
there
is still TIME.

clarissa pinkola estes

EVERYTHING tells me that i am about to make a WRONG decision, but making MISTAKES is just part of LIFE what does the world want of me? does it want me to take NO RISKS, to go back to where i came from because i didn't have the COURAGE to say "YES" to LIFE?

paulo coelho

YOU have the freedom to be YOUR SELF, your true self, HERE and NOW, and nothing can stand in your WAY.

richard bach

Listen —

are you BREATHING just a little, and calling it a LIFE?

mary oliver